COOL JOKES FOR

SUMMER

● LITTLE BOOK, ●
BIG LAUGHS

BY KIDS
FOR KIDS

Discover the
Oliver & Hope®
Storybook Series
at vhccf.org.

UnitedHealthcare
Children's Foundation®

ISBN: 978-0-692-60791-6

Manufactured in the United States of America.
First Printing.

Publisher: UHCCF/Adventure
Author: Meg Cadts and UHCCF
Contact: UnitedHealthcare
                  Children's Foundation

                  MN017-W400
                  P.O. Box 41
                  Minneapolis, MN 55440-0041

                  1-855-MY-UHCCF (1-855-698-4223)
                  uhccf.org

Now, this will make you smile.

Not only does this book deliver hours of good laughs, it also supports a good cause. All the jokes that appear in this book have been shared by kids through their parents, many of whom have a direct connection to the UnitedHealthcare Children's Foundation (UHCCF).

UHCCF, above all else, is about delivering smiles to children and families that need it most. Since 1999, that mission has been awarding thousands of medical grants, totaling tens of millions of dollars. The sale of this book helps make those medical grants possible. So remember when you're smiling your way through the following pages, you'll be helping so many more smile along with you.

About UHCCF

UHCCF is a 501(c)(3) charitable organization that provides medical grants to help children gain access to health-related services not covered, or not fully covered, by their family's commercial health insurance plan. Families can receive up to $5,000 annually per child ($10,000 lifetime maximum per child), and do not need to have insurance through UnitedHealthcare to be eligible. UHCCF was founded in 1999. Since 2007, UHCCF has awarded more than 14,000 grants valued at over $36M to children and their families across the United States. UHCCF's funding is provided by contributions from individuals, corporations and UnitedHealth Group employees. To apply, donate or learn more, please visit uhccf.org.

PRESENTED TO YOU BY:

TO: _____

From: _____

My Favorite Jokes Are On Pages:

_____

_____

What did the magician say to the fisherman?

"Pick a cod any cod."

Cole J. E. I Pittsburgh, PA

What kind of pet does the sun have?

A hot dog!

Isabella V. I Great Falls, MT

What do you call a witch who lives at the beach?

A sand-witch.

Levi C. I Beech Grove, IN

Knock Knock.

Who's there?

Interrupting cow.

Interrupting cow who?
(Mooo while they are talking)

Alexander T. I Chaska, MN

Why was the cat pacing in the grass?

She was meowing the lawn.

Peyton H. | Scottsdale, AZ

What does a cow wear on its face?

A moostache.

Camden G. | Maysville, KY

What did the ocean say to the boat?

Nothing, it waved.

Gigi G. | Lansdale, PA

Who do you call when your child is crying?

The whaaaa-mbulance.

Olivia H. | Rogers, MN

Why did the rubber chicken cross the road?

To get to the "rubber" side...

Jaden M. | Beaumont, TX

UnitedHealthcare
Children's Foundation

Why did the chicken cross the playground?

To get to the other slide!

Brooke D. | Boston, MA

What kind of cat likes his reflection?

A meerkat.

Olivia H. | Rogers, MN

How did the fish get to the battlefield?

In a tank.

Anonymous

Why did the pink panda go to the doctor?

Because she was pink!

Peyton H. | Scottsdale, AZ

If you don't feel well this summer, what do you probably have?

A pair of gloues on your hands!

Caleb E. | Greensboro, NC

What do you do for a blue whale?

Cheer him up!

Gracey W. | Mount Washington, KY

What's black, white, and red all over?

A Dalmatian with a sunburn!

Zoe B. | St. Louis Park, MN

What flowers grow between your nose and your chin?

Tulips.

Mackenzie D. | Cromwell, CT

What did one ocean do with the other ocean?

They waved.

Adam H. | Land O' Lakes, FL

Why was the bicycle leaning on the fence?

Because it was two-tired to stand up by itself!

James F. | Indianapolis, IN

What instrument do you find in a bathroom?

Tuba toothpaste!

Roshni R. | North Barrington, IL

Knock Knock.

Who's there?

Atch.

Atch who?

Bless you!

Cole H. | Minneapolis, MN

What did the head fly do when the other flies weren't working?

Fire-flies.

Zachary T. | Belmont, CA

How do you communicate with a fish?

Drop it a line.

Juldyz W. | Buffalo, MN

What do you call a boomerang that you throw and it doesn't come back?

A stick.

Evan M. | Albuquerque, NM

What is able to sit still in a corner, yet travel the world?

A stamp.

Luke M. | Hillsborough, NJ

Why is everyone so sad in the summer?

Because the sky is always so blue.

Lily C. | Lousiville, KY

Why is a koala bear not a real bear?

They don't have koala-fications!

Kaitlyn V. | Montrose, MN

Why couldn't the pirate learn the alphabet?

He gets lost at "C."

Makenzie R. | Burlington, NC

Why do bananas have to put on sunscreen before they go to the beach?

Because they might peel.

Elaina C. | Bridgeport, CT

How long are a pair of shoes?

Two feet!

Zachary T. | Belmont, CA

Did you hear about the fire at the circus?

It was "in tents."

Natalie M. | Apple Valley, MN

Why does an octopus laugh so hard?

They have ten-tickles (tentacles).

Loren H. | Waxhaw, NC

What did the frog say to the other frog?

"Don't be so jumpy!"

Adam H. | Land O' Lakes, FL

Knock Knock.

Who's there?

Cargo.

Cargo who?

Cargo beep beep.

Alexander C. | Winston Salem, NC

Why do doctors stay calm?

Because they have a lot of "patients."

Elliana D. | Duluth, MN

Why was the kid not too smart when he went to the beach?

Because when his mom told him to bring sunscreen, he took his computer monitor.

Emily B. | Louisville, KY

Do you want to hear a construction joke?

I'm still working on it.

Maddie Grace H. | Katy, TX

UnitedHealthcare Children's Foundation

What do you call a frog who parks illegally?

Toad!

(Towed)

Riley A. | Buffalo, NY

Knock Knock.

Who's there?

Silent Man.

Silent Man who?

..... (don't say anything)

Alexander C. | Winston Salem, NC

Why did the cow cross the road?

To get the chicken to moo-ve.

Dean M. | Apple Valley, MN

What do you call a magic owl?

WHOOO Dini!

Hadley N. | Bristol, TN

Why can't Dalmatians hide?

They are always spotted.

Kianna D. | Phoenix, AZ

What did the Pacific Ocean say to the Atlantic Ocean?

Nothing, it just waved!

Alice C. | New Prague, MN

Why did the mosquito cross the road?

He saw the blood bank across the street.

Avm B. | Tampa, FL

What runs faster on the beach; hot or cold?

Hot, because you can always catch a cold!

Anshul N. | Springfield, IL

How do billboards talk?

Sign language.

A'Nya T. | Lexington, NC

UnitedHealthcare
Children's Foundation

Why did Cinderella get kicked off the baseball team?

She kept running away from the ball!

Emma H. | White House, TN

What did the Wicked Witch of the West say at the beach?

"Hello, Sandwich (Sand Witch), it's hot here and I'm melting!"

Aidan L. | Edgerton, KS

Where does Darth Vader work in New York City?

The EMPIRE State Building.

Landon L. | Saint Johns, FL

Knock Knock.

Who's there?

Boo.

Boo who?

Don't cry, it's just a joke!

Lindsey C. | New Prague, MN

Why did the chicken cross the road twice?

To prove he wasn't a chicken.

Caleb W. l Las Vegas, NV

What did the letter say to the stamp?

"Stick with me and you'll go places."

Makenzie R. l Burlington, NC

Where is a cow's favorite place to go on summer vacation?

Moo York!

Madelyn W. l Saint Michael, MN

What kind of vitamins does a fish take?

Vitamin sea.

Gracey W. l Mount Washington, KY

Why don't bears wear shoes?

Because they are bear-footed!

Claire C. l Hattiesburg, MS

UnitedHealthcare
Children's Foundation

What word starts with an "E", ends with an "E" and only has one letter in it?

An envelope.

Zachary T. | Belmont, CA

What has two banks but no money?

A river.

A'Nya T. | Lexington, NC

Your eyes look droopy, are you sleepy?

Well, my eyes are sleepy, but I'm not.

Noah F. | San Antonio, TX

Why do sharks swim in saltwater?

Because pepper water makes them sneeze.

Mason C. | Mabelvale, AR

Why do you never see elephants hiding in trees?

Because they are really good at it.

Andrew V. | Green Bay, WI

What kind of bees never die?

Zom-bees.

Andrew V. | Green Bay, WI

What does the sun drink out of?

Sunglasses.

Mia T. | The Woodlands, TX

What did Adele say when she crossed the road?

"Hello from the other side."

Cruz V. | Mesa, AZ

What do frogs like to drink on a hot summer day?

Croak-O-Cola.

Alyssa S. | Denham Springs, LA

I called our local zoo to see if they were open, but I couldn't get through because their lion was busy.

Araya L. | Frederick, MD

Why was it hot after a baseball game?

All of the fans left.

Jack V. | Sobieski, WI

Where are pencils made?

Pennsylvania.

Joshua W. | Manchester, CT

What did the beach say to the wave?

"Long tide no see!"

Arnav N. | Springfield, IL

What did the traffic light say to the car?

"Don't look, I'm changing."

Josie H. | Kent, UK

Why did the cow dress like a chicken?

So he could cross the road!

Hannah L. | St. Louis Park, MN

What is a sleeping person's favorite thing to do under water?

Snore-keling.

Aarnav K. | Nashville, TN

How do trees access the internet?

They "log" on!

Madison M. | Las Vegas, NV

What did the janitor say when she jumped out of the closet?

"Supplies!"

Zabella G. | Devine, TX

What did the softball glove say to the softball?

"Catch you later!"

Gianna S. | East Haven, CT

Why is it impossible to run in a campground?

You can only ran because it's past tents.

Tony W. | Buffalo, MN

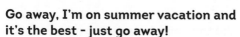

Knock Knock.

Who's there?

Summer vacation.

Summer vacation who?

Go away, I'm on summer vacation and it's the best - just go away!

Taryn W. I Barnum, MN

Where did the horse go when he lost his tail?

The retail store.

Gabby G. I Tampa, FL

Where do ghosts like to go swimming?

Lake "Eerie!"

Evie H. I Fishers, IN

Knock Knock.

Who's there?

Ya.

Ya who?

You don't have to get so excited.

Zoe C. I Sacramento, CA

What do you call a snowman in July?

A puddle.

Aditya V. | Basking Ridge, NJ

Why did the cantaloupe jump into the lake?

It wanted to be a watermelon.

Blake C. | Columbia, TN

What detergent do swimmers use to wash their swimsuit?

Tide.

Sophie H. | Fishers, IN

Where does a penguin store its money?

In a snow bank.

Lauren V. | Castleton, NY

Did you hear the joke about the jump rope?

"Ahhhh skip it!"

Gerek T. | Duluth, MN

UnitedHealthcare Children's Foundation

Where do crayons go on vacation?

Color-ado!

Lily H. | Fishers, IN

What's harder to catch the faster you run?

Your breath.

Kayla M. | Baxter, TN

What is black, white, and red all over?

A sunburned zebra.

Alyssa S. | Denham Springs, LA

What is brown and sticky?

A stick.

Joshua W. | Manchester, CT

What did the zero say to the eight?

"Nice belt."

Aaron K. | Waconia, MN

What is at the end of a rainbow?

A "w."

Adelaide G. | Grand Junction, CO

Where does Noah keep his bees?

The Ark hives.

Gabby G. | Tampa, FL

What kind of crows stick together?

Vel-crows.

Joshua M. | Edina, MN

How did the farmer find his wife?

He tractor-ed her down.

Thomas N. | Thurmont, MD

What animal jumps higher than a tree?

All animals jump higher than a tree; trees can't jump!

Anonymous

UnitedHealthcare
Children's Foundation

So did you hear what the cowboy asked his horse?

"Why the long face?"

Anonymous

What do sheep do on sunny days?

Have a baa-baa-cue.

Taylor N. | Saint Augustine, FL

Knock Knock.

Who's there?

Don't-get-the-flu.

Don't-get-the-flu who?

Good advice! Don't get the flu!

Revaya D. | St. Louis Park, MN

What did the football say to the bank?

"Can I have my quarter back?"

Zabella G. | Devine, TX

Knock Knock.

Who's there?

Woo.

Woo who?

Don't get so excited, it's just a joke.

Sawyer G. | Saint Louis, MO

What has four wheels and flies?

A garbage truck!

Eli C. | Mesa, AZ

Why did the dinosaur take a shower?

Because he exSTINKED.

Evan C. | Farmington, MN

Knock Knock.

Who's there?

Barbie.

Barbie who?

Barbie-q-chicken.

Alaina H. | East Haven, CT

What does a vegetable wear to the beach?

A zucchini!

Megan P. | Islip, NY

Where do goldfish go on summer vacation?

Around the globe.

Amayah J. | Palm Bay, FL

Why did the circle graduate college early?

Because he had 360 degrees.

Ethan F. | Carthage, NC

What happens when a frog's car breaks down?

It gets toad (towed) away.

Harley W. | Pittsburgh, PA

A cowboy rides into town on Friday, he stays for three days and leaves on Friday. How did he do it?

The horse's name is Friday.

Chloe K. | Carver, MN

How do you make time fly?

Throw a clock out the window.

Jackson S. | Lilburn, GA

Why do cows have bells?

Because they don't have horns!

Jace J. | Fishers, IN

Knock Knock.

Who's there?

Dwayne.

Dwayne who?

Dwayne the bathtub!

Daniel W. | St. Louis Park, MN

How does a penguin build its home?

Igloos it together.

Benjamin H. | Oroville, CA

What runs, but never walks, has a bed, but never sleeps, has a mouth, but never eats?

A river.

Jacob A. | Wausau, WI

Do you know why Super Mario doesn't wear shorts?

He prefers... denim, denim, denim.

Konnor P. | Ft. Worth, TX

Where do you put a noisy dog?

In a barking lot!

Anonymous

Why did the golfer wear two pairs of pants?

Because he got a hole in one.

Juldyz W. | Buffalo, MN

Why did the teacher wear sunglasses?

Because her class was so bright!

Ethan L. | Phoenix, AZ

Why do superstars need fans?

To be cool.

Sophia C. | Cypress, CA

What do dogs eat to cool themselves off in the summer?

Pupsicles.

James O. | Wauwatosa, WI

What do you get when you combine a fish and an elephant?

Swim trunks!

Abby B. | Chaska, MN

What do bees chew?

Bumble gum!

Megan P. | Islip, NY

What did the bike trail say to the shoes?

"Go take a hike."

James O. | Wauwatosa, WI

How do you catch a squirrel?

Climb a tree and act like a nut.

Isaiah G. | Melrose, MN

How does NASA take vacation?

They planet!

Amanda W. | Alpharetta, GA

What do you call a deer with no eyes?

"I have no eye dear!"

Eleni A. | Tarpon Springs, FL

Why are road trips dangerous?

Because it hurts to "hit" the road!

Mackenzie L. | Carlsbad, CA

What is a baby's favorite kind of exercise?

Spit-ups!

Adrien Z. | Three Bridges, NJ

Where do sharks go on vacation?

Finland!

Makena M. | Glendale, AZ

Why did the baseball player get sent to jail?

Because he was caught stealing second base.

Issac B. | Bellflower, CA

Why wouldn't the egg cross the road?

Because he was a chicken.

Tristan S. | Bayport, MN

What kind of shoes do ninjas wear?

Sneakers.

Fred G. | Tampa, FL

UnitedHealthcare
Children's Foundation

Why did the turkey cross the road?

It was the chicken's day off!

Archie E. | St. Louis Park, MN

What did the pig in the desert say?

"Hey guys, I'm bacon out here."

Olivia S. | Adkins, TX

What goes "Ha ha plop?"

A kid laughing his head off!

Nolan L. | Foster, RI

What do you call an alligator in a vest?

An in-vest-igator!

Sydney Z. | Lehigh Acres, FL

What is hard to find, but easy to lose, worth more than gold, but not a cent?

Friends.

Cody L. | Tolland, CT

What did one pool noodle say to the other?

"Look at me, I can do the wave!"

Hayden W. I Van Alstyne, TX

Why did the man love his barbeque?

Because it was the grill of his dreams!

Andy M. I Damascus, OR

Where do mummies go swimming?

The Dead Sea.

Malachi M. I Chico, CA

Where does a frog fly his flag?

On a tadpole.

A'Nya T. I Lexington, NC

Why did the horse cross the road?

Because it wasn't stable.

Olivia P. I Brooklyn Park, MN

A lady told her neighbor, "I went to the animal shelter yesterday and got a puppy for my son."

The neighbor said, "That was really a good swap!"

Sowmya G. | Tampa, FL

What did the octopus say to his girlfriend?

"Can I hold your hand, hand, hand, hand, hand, hand, hand, hand?"

Jordan L. | Schofield, WI

What dog sweats in the summer?

A hot dog!

Mayla T. | Golden Valley, MN

What do you get with a fly, a pet, and a car?

A flying car-pet.

A'Nya T. | Lexington, NC

Why do kittens make the best pets?

Because they are PURRRRFECT.

Leo H. | Allentown, PA

What did the flying squirrel say to the flying lizard?

"Do you want to play glide and seek?"

Brooklyn L. | Duluth, MN

What do you call a first baseman who drops the ball?

Benched.

Zachary W. | Dearing, GA

Where does a general keep his armies?

Up his sleevies!

Silvio C. | Naperville, IL

What day does a chicken hate?

Friday!

Reagan H. | Plano, TX

Did you hear the one about the evil sheep?

He tried to wool the world.

Morgan L. | Greensboro, NC

Why did the cookie go to the doctor?

It felt crummy.

Evie H. | Fishers, IN

What do you get when you mix a duck and a calculator?

A quackulator!

Ethan B. | Eagan, MN

What does a bee do when it's hot?

He takes off his yellow jacket.

Andy M. | Damascus, OR

What do cows read in the morning?

A moos-paper.

Kelsey L. | Ocean Isle Beach, NC

Why did the dog sit on the watch?

He wanted to be a watchdog.

Bryce H. | Sugar Land, TX

What is it called when the Minnesota state bird flies in front of the moon?

A loon-ar eclipse.

Samantha C. | Minneapolis, MN

Why did the house go to the doctor?

It had window panes.

Jack V. | Sobieski, WI

What do you call a helper with a sour attitude?

Lemon-aide.

Abri N. | Redondo Beach, CA

What do you call an animal that lives on land?

A land-imal.

Emily S. | San Antonio, TX

What is a cow's favorite game to play?

Moosical chairs.

Morgan L. | Greensboro, NC

What is better than a talking horse?

A spelling bee.

Sofia R. | Victoria, MN

What did the duck say when he went into the drug store?

"Please give me some Chapstick, and put it on my bill."

Luciana L. | Cleveland, OH

What did the cow say to his friend when he got scared by a mouse?

"You are such a COWard!"

Landyn J. | San Antonio, TX

What do you call a bunch of rabbits walking backwards?

A receding hairline.

Jaidyn J. | Delaware, OH

Knock Knock.

Who's there?

Cow.

Cow who?

Cow moooo!

McKenzie S. | Waconia, MN

Why was the report card all wet?

Because all the grades were below "C" level.

Allison M. | Damascus, OR

Why did the detective duck cross the road?

To quack the case of the missing pool.

Y.L. | Winston Salem, NC

Why do underwater creatures read a lot of history books?

They are very so-fish-ticated.

Caitlyn I. | Salem, NH

What is big, red, and eats rocks?

A big red rock eater.

Genna J. | Plymouth, MN

Which flower gives the best kisses?

A tulip.

Kelsey L. | Ocean Isle Beach, NC

Why did the cow cross the road?

It was the chicken's day off.

Amos J. | Burnettsville, IN

Where do cars go swimming?

In a car pool.

Luke B. | Foothill Ranch, CA

What do you call a huge pile of cats?

A meowtain!

Joseph L. | Glenside, PA

What's a flower's favorite animal?

A dande-lion!

Caitlyn I. | Salem, NH

What do you do if someone rolls their eyes at you?

You pick them up and roll them right back.

Max E. | Phoenix, AZ

What do you call a daddy balloon?

Pops.

Abri N. | Redondo Beach, CA

What is gray and has four legs and a trunk?

A mouse on vacation.

Allison M. | Damascus, OR

Knock Knock.

Who's there?

I don't know, you asked me!

Brayden G. | Minneapolis, MN

UnitedHealthcare Children's Foundation

Which summer months have 28 days?

All of them.

Hailey A. | Chaska, MN

What do you call a bull that is bad at everything?

Terribull.

Zachary C. | Warminster, PA

Why did the girl put lipstick all over her forehead?

So she could makeup her mind.

Montrose B. | Chicago, IL

Two hats were sitting on the beach enjoying the warm weather. One hat said to the other, "You stay here, I'll go on a head."

Will S. | Pasadena, MD

What time does Sean Connery get to Wimbledon?

Tennish.

Ja'meire M. | Frederick, MD

Where does a 600-pound gorilla go?

Anywhere it wants.

Genna J. | Plymouth, MN

What do you call an elephant in a phone booth?

Stuck.

Ella L. | Falls Church, VA

What is the tallest building in the world?

A library, because it has so many stories.

Drake K. | Wausau, WI

Where does Tarzan go on vacation?

Hollywood and Vine.

Z.L. | Winston Salem, NC

UnitedHealthcare Children's Foundation

What do you say to a hitch-hiking frog?

"Hop in!"

Andy M. | Damascus, OR

What does Spiderman say he does for a living?

He's a web designer.

Morgan L. | Greensboro, NC

What do you call a fish with no eye?

FSH!

Joseph L. | Glenside, PA

What do you call a crab with a crown?

A pinch-ess!

Chloe U. | Moline, IL

How do you make a goldfish age?

Take away the "g."

Larkin B. | Eden Prairie, MN

Why was the lawnmower so tired?

Because it took a lawn time!

Aryan P. | Shakopee, MN

What did the princess glove say to the baseball bat?

"I need to get to the ball."

Noah H. | Clermont, FL

Why did the cheerleader put extra salt on her food in the summer?

She wanted to do summer salts.

Makena F. | Redondo Beach, CA

Knock Knock.

Who's there?

Calful.

Calful who?

You have to be calf-ful when you're near a cow.

Brayden D. | Coventry, CT

Knock Knock.

Who's there?

Hatch.

Hatch who?

Oh, bless you!

Tatiana H. | Las Vegas, NV

Where do fish hide when it rains?

They don't! They are already wet!

Leen A. | Orange, CA

How do bears keep their den cool in the summer?

Bear conditioning.

Y. L. | Winston Salem, NC

What did the buffalo say at camp drop off?

"Bison."

Charlotte C. | Saint Paul, MN

What do you get when you mix a sheep and porcupine?

A nicely knitted sweater.

Morgan L. | Greensboro, NC

Why are fish so smart?

Because they live in schools!

Zachary T. | Belmont, CA

Why is the zebra striped?

Because it didn't want to be spotted.

Deepak K. | Eden Prairie, MN

Knock Knock.

Who's there?

Pasture.

Pasture who?

It's pasture bedtime.

Lyra F. | Pittsburgh, PA

What did the fancy airplane say to the other airplane?

"You look too plain."

Anoushka K. | Richmond Hill, GA

Knock Knock.

Who's there?

Doctor.

Doctor who?

Exactly.

Susanna C. | Saint Paul, MN

What did one firefly say to the other firefly?

"I have to glow now!"

Samantha S. | Greenwood, IN

I'm sorry I wrecked your car, but I wanted to see how a Mercedes Benz.

Ghabriel S. | Neosho, MO

Why did Mickey Mouse go to outer space?

He was looking for Pluto.

Elizabeth F. | Wharton, NJ

If Anna from Frozen married Ben, what would you call the couple?

Ben-Anna.

Leen A. | Orange, CA

What happens when a lumberjack goes swimming?

He gets waterlogged!

Jacob R. | Casa Grande, AZ

Knock Knock.

Who's there?

Knock Knock.

Knock Knock who?

Why are you knocking at me? This is my joke!

Caiden M. | Eden Prairie, MN

UnitedHealthcare Children's Foundation

How do you wake up Lady Gaga?

You Poker Face!

Jacob R. | Casa Grande, AZ

Why couldn't the pony sing himself a lullaby?

He was a little hoarse.

Lisa W. | Hesperia, CA

Why couldn't the pirate go to the movies?

Because it was rated "R."

Anonymous

What did the canoe say to the other canoe?

"Canoe (can you) float?"

Kali S. | Delano, MN

There were ten cats on a boat and one jumped off. How many were left?

There were none! They were all a bunch of copy cats!

Jack B. | Boise, ID

What's a movie's favorite camping grounds?

Holly Woods.

Avery C. | Clearwater, FL

I was going to tell you an airplane joke, but it's way over your head.

Yszabehl S. | Neosho, MO

What did the two roads say to each other?

"Hi-way!"

Zachary T. | Belmont, CA

Why did the rabbit cross the road?

To show his girlfriend he could hip hop.

Torben N. | Plymouth, MN

What did one tide pool say to another?

"Show me your mussels!"

Zoee R. | Superior, WI

UnitedHealthcare
Children's Foundation

Why was the math book so sad?

Because it had too many problems.

Raphael V. | Huntington Beach, CA

Where does a cow like to go to cool off in the summer?

To the moooo-vie theater!

Sophie E. | Ham Lake, MN

Knock Knock.

Who's there?

Sleeping Beauty.

Sleeping Beauty who?

Snores...

Lisa W. | Hesperia, CA

When is a car not a car?

When it turns into a driveway.

Dareyon B. | Danville, VA

What is worse than raining cats and dogs?

Hailing taxis.

Daymian H. | Orland Park, IL

What did the shovel say to the sand bucket?

"I dig you!"

Ella Jean A. | Germantown, TN

What is a pirate's favorite letter?

You think it would be "R" but it be the "C."

Nathan J. | South Haven, MN

What do you use to do laundry while on summer vacation on a cruise ship?

Tide-tanic.

Lily C. | Lousiville, KY

What's green and loud?

A froghorn.

Jack B. | Germantown, TN

What did the tie say to the hat?

"You go on a head and I'll hang around."

Gabriel V. | Huntington Beach, CA

Why can a chicken coop only have two doors?

Because if it had four it would be a chicken sedan.

Avry R. | Kingsport, TN

What does a boat do when it's sick?

It goes to the dock.

Mia T. | The Woodlands, TX

What does not get wet when it rains?

The ocean.

Dalton M. | Hiltons, VA

What summer flower is king of the yard?

The dandelion!

Isabelle S. | Minnetonka, MN

How do you cut a wave in half?

Use a sea saw.

Blake C. | Columbia, TN

What do cats call mice on skateboards?

Meals on Wheels!

Zoee R. | Superior, WI

What kind of bedtime stories do cows read?

Dairy tales.

Morgan L. | Greensboro, NC

Why did Humpty Dumpty have a great fall?

To make up for his miserable summer vacation!

Jackson S. | Woodbury, MN

What did the pig say at the beach on a hot summer's day?

"I'm bacon!"

Sophie H. | Fishers, IN

What's the best thing about Switzerland?

I don't know but their flag is a big plus.

Lillian C. | North Huntingdon, PA

What do you get when you cross a porcupine with a sheep?

An animal that knits its own sweater.

Elycia B. | Oklahoma City, OK

Why are frogs so happy?

Because they eat whatever bugs them.

Vivaan B. | Chanhassen, MN

What is the only dinosaur that likes to golf?

A TEE-Rex.

Marleigh S. | Falling Waters, WV

How did the barber win the race?

Because he knew a short cut.

Chris S. | Basking Ridge, NJ

Knock Knock.

Who's there?

Hoo.

Hoo who?

You talk like an owl!

Timothy S. | Eau Claire, WI

What do you call a skunk that flies?

A smellicopter!

Briden S. | Orlando, FL

Why is Cinderella so bad at baseball?

Because her coach was a pumpkin.

Kaylin G. | Waconia, MN

If you work as a security guard at a Samsung store, does that make you the Guardian of the Galaxy?

Jay B. | Cincinnati, OH

/ UnitedHealthcare Children's Foundation

What is the best day to go to the beach?

SUNday.

Sophia D. | Galena, OH

What's red and smells like blue paint?

Red paint.

Olivia H. | Rogers, MN

Knock Knock.

Who's there?

Leaf.

Leaf who?

Leaf me alone.

Avah C. | Stoddard, WI

What do you call a greedy crab?

Shellfish.

Justice R. | New Orleans, LA

Why can't spiders be pilots?

Because they only know how to tailspin.

Hunter N. | Bloomington, MN

I had a wooden whistle and it wooden whistle. I had a steel whistle, and I steel couldn't whistle... I have a tin whistle... now I tin whistle!

Lauren R. | Mason, OH

What did the Earth say to the grass?

"You are grounded."

Timothy P. | Laurence Harbor, NJ

Knock Knock.

Who's there?

I'm.

I'm who?

You don't even know your name?

Avah C. | Stoddard, WI

UnitedHealthcare
Children's Foundation

What is white, black and red all over?

A sunburned penguin.

Emma P. | Kettering, OH

Why did the nose walk across the road?

Because it didn't want to run!

Austin V. | Corpus Christi, TX

What does one pencil say to another pencil?

"Looking sharp!"

Ambika B. | Chanhassen, MN

What animal is best at hitting a baseball?

A bat.

Kadin S. | Huntington Beach, CA

What do you call an electric parrot?

A shock-a-too.

Lillian C. | North Huntingdon, PA

What did the snail say when he was riding on the turtle's back?

"WEEEEEEEEEEEEEEEEEEEEEEEEEEEEEEEEEE!"

Chloe W. | Morristown, TN

Knock Knock.

Who's there?

Donahue.

Donahue who?

Donahue knock again.

Desiree W. | Gainesville, FL

A horse walked into an ice cream shop and the cashier asked, "Why the long face?"

Joshua D. | Eden Prairie, MN

Why did the Boy Scout bury the flashlight?

Because its batteries were dead.

Cody G. | Eau Claire, WI

What did one eye say to the other eye?

"Don't look now, but something between us smells."

Jackson T. | Naugatuck, CT

What did the tree wear to the pool party?

Swimming trunks!

Lauren D. | Lexington, KY

What sound does a piggy bank make?

Coink-coink!

Silas R. | St. Paul, MN

What did the talking cat say to the other cat while he was doing a back flip?

"That was "meow"some!"

Elliot S. | Indianapolis, IN

How do crabs call each other across the bay?

They use their shell phones.

Damaris C. | Maricopa, AZ

What do you call a bear with no socks?

Bear foot!

Isabella S. | Superior, WI

Why did the cow cross the road?

To go to the mooo-uie theater.

Ryan W. | Rosemount, MN

It's summer, so why did the goose cross the road?

Because the chicken went on summer vacation and got fried!

Lily F. | DeLand, FL

What has four legs and no eyes?

A table.

Brooks C. | Waverly, IA

What type of clothes do clouds wear?

Thunderwear.

Elloree K. | Goose Creek, SC

What can run, but never walk, has a mouth, but never talks, has a head, but never weeps, and has a bed, but never sleeps?

A river!

Samson G. | Saint Louis, MO

What does a cat like to eat on a hot summer day?

A mice cream cone.

Callie M. | Eden Prairie, MN

Knock Knock.

Who's there?

Anya.

Anya who?

Anya back is a hairy spider!

Paige K. | Pulaski, WI

What do call an alligator that helps teachers out at school?

A Gatorade.

Avion I. | Murfreesboro, TN

Have you ever seen a hippo hiding in a tree?

See, they are really good at it!

Alex T. | Minneapolis, MN

What is a cow's favorite subject?

Moo-sic.

Elycia B. | Oklahoma City, OK

Do you know what IDK means?

I don't know.

Oh man, no one knows!

Alex V. | Adel, IA

How do you catch a whole school of fish?

With bookworms!

Elliott T. | Greenfield, WI

Why did the farmer cross the road?

To get the chicken back!

Emerson K. | Franklin, OH

UnitedHealthcare
Children's Foundation

Why did the computer go to the doctor?

Because it had a virus!

John C. | Hudson, FL

What is a grasshopper's favorite sport?

Cricket.

Malia M. | Windsor, CT

What can you wear everyday and it never goes out of style?

A smile.

Serenity H. | Meadowlands, MN

Knock Knock.

Who's there?

Armageddon.

Armageddon who?

Arm-a-getting out of here!

Luke P. | Morgantown, WV

If Washington's wife went to Washington, while Washington's wash woman washed Washington's clothes, how many washes in all?

There are no washes in the word "all."

Sarah P. | Oroville, CA

Why did the bird go to the doctor?

To get tweet-ment.

Vanessa R. | Plano, TX

Why did the monster not eat the basketball?

Because it tasted flat.

Isaiah G. | Melrose, MN

Why did the chicken cross the road?

To get to your house.

Knock Knock.

Who's there?

Bock, bock, bock (chicken noise).

Briana P. | Bristol, CT

Where do all the Star Wars characters go shopping?

Darth Maul.

Noah R. | Lake Dallas, TX

What's a puppy say when he sits on sandpaper?

"Ruff!"

Scarlett P. | Plymouth, MN

Why are hippos so wrinkly?

Because you can't iron them.

Paige T. | Iron River, WI

Which baseball player holds water?

The pitcher!

Nolan R. | Clarksville, TN

What do you get if you cross a parrot with a centipede?

A walkie-talkie.

Cayera H. | Republic, MO

Why can't the pirate play cards?

Because he was sitting on the deck!

Winslow R. | Plano, TX

Why did the cowboy buy a wiener dog?

Somebody told him to "get along little doggie!"

Jack B. | Boise, ID

What did the cat say?

He said he was puuuurrrrrfect.

Samuel E. | Glendale, AZ

What do you call it when the alpacas take over the world?

The Alpacacalypse.

Emily G. | Blaine, MN

UnitedHealthcare
Children's Foundation

Why did the farmer win the award at the county fair?

Because he was out standing in his field!

Porter J. | Maple Grove, MN

Where does Batman take a shower?

In the batroom.

Mac F. | Thousand Oaks, CA

How did the cow pay for his summer vacation?

With lots of moo-ney.

Lana M. | Middletown, DE

What do you call a French guy in sandals?

Phillipe Phloppe.

Arnav B. | Ellicott City, MD

What do you call a singing computer?

A-Dell.

Daniel V. | Stafford, TX

When does it rain money?

When the weather changes!

Noah W. | Magalia, CA

What did the cow say to the chicken?

"Moooooove out of the way."

Anonymous

Where do eggs go on summer vacation?

New Yolk City.

Tony W. | Buffalo, MN

What fish only swims at night?

A starfish.

Emma H. | Austin, IN

How do you keep warm in a cold room?

You go to the corner because it is always 90 degrees.

Ian S. | Denham Springs, LA

What is a pirate's favorite class?

Aaarrrrt class.

Kaydence B. | Glendale, AZ

What kind of turtle flies?

A turtle dove.

Grace C. | Independence, MO

Why did the duck cross the swimming pool?

To get to the sunscreen on the other side.

Mckenna C. | Plymouth, MN

How do you track Will Smith in the woods?

Look for his Fresh Prince.

Joseph D. | Westerville, OH

What did the painter do when she got cold?

Put on another coat!

Noah L. | Fairfax, VA

Knock Knock.

Who's there?

Canoe.

Canoe who?

Can you come out and play with me?

Ivy G. | Brigham City, UT

What goes zzub zzub?

A bee flying backward.

Anonymous

What do you get when you throw a book into the ocean?

A title wave.

Daniel H. | Lexington, NC

Why do cats like really neat things?

Because they like everything purrrrrfect!

Eliora E. | St. Louis Park, MN

There are three copy cats on a plane and one jumps out, how many are left?

None, they are all copy cats.

Anthony S. | La Habra, CA

What kind of books does the solar system like to read on a summer vacation?

Comet books.

Jordan N. | Milwaukee, WI

What does a Norwegian dog say?

"Woof-da."

Isabelle E. | Minneapolis, MN

Knock Knock.

Who's there?

Little Old Lady!

Little Old Lady who?

I didn't know you could yodel!

Hailey A. | Cape Girardeau, MO

A cat fell and hit his head. The cat's owner took him to the veterinarian and asked "Is there a MRI for cats?" The doctor answered, "You mean a Cat Scan?"

Matthew M. | Deer Park, TX

What falls down but never falls up?

The rain.

Mia R. | Duluth, MN

What state has the most cows?

Moo York.

Morgan L. | Greensboro, NC

Why did the little boy think it was ok to litter?

Because he saw a road sign that said "Fine For Littering".

Sandhra T. | Cheshire, CT

What did one wall say to the other wall?

"I'll meet you at the corner!"

Linda M. | Phoenix, AZ

UnitedHealthcare Children's Foundation

What do you call a Black-eyed Susan without the dark center of the flower?

Susan.

Joshua C. | Farmington, MN

What do you call a pencil with no point?

Quit thinking about it, there's no point.

Avion I. | Murfreesboro, TN

Why was the store owner giving away used batteries?

Because they were free of charge!

Rayln M. | Magnolia, TX

What kind of bird never needs a haircut?

A Bald Eagle!

Ryder W. | La Mesa, CA

Why did the pelican get kicked out of the restaurant?

Because he had a big bill.

Hailey B. | Athens, WI

What did the ocean say to the umbrella?

Nothing, it just waved!

Maci B. | Denton, MD

Why does it get so hot in the stadium after the game?

Because all the fans left!

Nick B. | Warrington, PA

What did the farmer say when he lost his tractor?

"Where's my tractor?"

Jamie M. | Honolulu, HI

Knock Knock.

Who's there?

Owls.

Owls who?

They sure do!

Easton A. | Delano, MN

What whistles and runs, but doesn't talk?

A train.

Kylie R. | Shakopee, MN

Why did the dog sit in the shade?

He did not want to be a hot dog.

Zayda L. | Scottsdale, AZ

What is the perfect fish to catch?

An ANGELfish.

Lily C. | Lousiville, KY

Why did the horse keep falling over?

It just wasn't stable!

Jack B. | Boise, ID

What did the Lion King say to Simba when he was moving too slow?

"MOVE FASSA!"

Maya B. | Bristow, VA

How do you count cows?

With a cowculator.

Alycia D. | Lewisburg, TN

Why did the picture go to jail?

Because it was framed.

Tim L. | Champlin, MN

Why did the gum cross the road?

It was stuck to the chicken's foot.

Kadin S. | Huntington Beach, CA

What happens when you throw a green rock into the Red Sea?

It gets wet.

Matthew B. | Columbia, SC

Why does Peter Pan always fly?

Because he Neverlands.

Adrienne B. | Las Vegas, NV

Where is the warmest spot outside when it is 0 degrees?

In a 90 degree corner.

Lauren Z. | Merrill, WI

What did the tired slug say to the other slug?

"I'm feeling sluggish today."

Seth B. | Las Vegas, NV

How do you prevent a summer cold?

You catch it in the winter.

Zurrie L. | Scottsdale, AZ

What does Luke Skywalker drive?

Toy Yoda... and when it breaks down, Ewoks.

Connor N. | Kingsport, TN

Why do birds fly south for the winter?

Because it's too far to walk.

Randall C. | Shakopee, MN

What kind of dog likes to take baths the most?

A shampoo-dle.

Amanda T. | West Des Moines, IA

What kind of horse only comes out at night?

A night mare!

Isabella V. | Torrance, CA

What is the favorite game of cows playing in a field?

Moo-sical chairs.

Amelia B. | St. Louis Park, MN

Why was the monkey wearing green swimming trunks?

Because his blue ones were dirty!

Christopher S. | Nashville, TN

What washes up on the shores of tiny beaches?

Microwaves.

Delia K. | Sobieski, WI

Why don't mummies go on summer vacation?

They are afraid to relax and unwind.

Brody S. | Woodbury, MN

What do you call a field full of eyeballs?

An eye-patch.

Max N. | Frisco, TX

Knock Knock.

Who's there?

Knock Knock.

Who's there?

Knock Knock.

Who's there?

What do you mean? My name is Knock Knock!

Oliver S. | Des Moines, IA

Why did the sun not go to a university?

Because it had too many degrees.

Keira I. | Chalfont, PA

Knock Knock.

Who's there?

Nonna.

Nonna who?

Nonna your business.

Claira P. | Wausau, WI

What has four eyes but can't see?

Mississippi.

Mason R. | Victoria, MN

A man goes to his doctor and says, "Doctor, I am so confused. I lay awake at night and wonder if I am a wigwam or a teepee."

The doctor thinks for a minute and says, "I've got it! You're too tents (tense)!"

Claire B. | New Albany, OH

Why is the letter 'a' like a flower?

Because there is always a bee following it.

Alayna A. | Wichita, KS

UnitedHealthcare Children's Foundation

What did the moon say to the sun?

"Can you give my shoes a sun shine?"

Timothy C. | Dane, WI

What do you call a big cat that can't hear?

Def Leppard.

Gracey W. | Mount Washington, KY

Knock Knock.

Who's there?

Cow.

Cow who?

No silly, cows say moo!

Castiel K. | Blaine, MN

How did Harry Potter go down the hill?

He walked.

Nathan E. | Springville, UT

Why did the music teacher need a ladder?

To reach the high notes.

Gigi M. | Pepperell, MA

Last night I dreamt I was walking on a sandy beach... that explains the footprints in the litter box this morning!

Ocean C. | Vincennes, IN

What did the spider do on the computer?

Made a website.

Oliver S. | Des Moines, IA

What is a sheep's favorite summer activity?

Baaaaaaa-sketball.

Khloe A. | San Antonio, TX

Why did the cat run away from the tree?

It was afraid of its bark.

Sara E. | Plymouth, MN

How do birds talk to each other?

Through Twitter!

Kylie F. | Andover, MN

What do you call a purse with no price?

Priceless.

Sidd C. | Rochester, MI

Knock Knock.

Who's there?

Bam!

Bam who?

It's not bam-who, it's bamboo!

Oliver S. | Des Moines, IA

Why do elephants enjoy swimming in the summer?

They love to show off their trunks.

Nicholas S. | Wesley Chapel, FL

Why did the runner put a net on her head?

To catch her breath.

Avery C. | Onaslaska, WI

What do you call two doctors standing next to each other?

A pair-of-medics.

Aiden C. | Charlestown, IN

What gets wetter the more it dries?

A towel.

Mia T. | The Woodlands, TX

What do you call a pig that drives dangerously?

Road hog.

Elycia B. | Oklahoma City, OK

Why does Waldo wear stripes?

He doesn't want to be spotted!

Jessica D. | Eden Prairie, MN

UnitedHealthcare
Children's Foundation

What do you call a bull that is sleeping?

A bulldozer.

OnaRae L. | Rothschild, WI

Why doesn't Batman take Robin fishing?

Because he's afraid he will eat all of the worms!

Nathaniel B. | Katy, TX

An elephant, bear, and zebra went to a restaurant on their summer trip. They all had good food and now it is time to pay the bill. Can you guess who paid the bill?

The elephant. It was the only animal in the group that had trunks to hold his wallet.

Mithul V. | Plymouth, MN

Why did the seagull fly over the bay?

So it could be a bagel.

Camden G. | Maysville, KY

What did the bread say on a summer day?

"I'm toasted."

Jude S. | Redmond, WA

Do you need an Ark?

I Noah guy.

Kaden C. | Burlington, KY

What is it called when two fingers talk to each other?

Snapchat.

Jordynn D. | Eden Prairie, MN

Knock Knock.

Who's there?

Nana.

Nana who?

Nana Boo Boo!

Leah G. | Las Vegas, NV

What do you call a quiet sheep?

A shhhhhhhhheep.

Morgan L. | Greensboro, NC

What did one wave say to the other wave?

"Sea ya later!"

Gia B. | Kingston, NY

What does a pirate say if he drives any type of vehicle?

"Carrr!"

Deepak K. | Eden Prairie, MN

How do cows do most of their shopping?

They use cattle-ogs!

Grace F. | Agawam, MA

Why is the letter "t" like an island?

Because it is in the middle of water.

Oliver S. | Des Moines, IA

What is a cow's favorite place to go on vacation?

MOOOO York!

Hailey G. | Wake Forest, NC

Who is the chicken's favorite basketball player?

Charles Baak-ley.

Brady M. | Phoenix, AZ

What do you call Batman and Robin after they get run over by a steam roller?

Flatman and Ribbon!

Carter K. | Lombard, IL

What is a frog's favorite type of music?

Hip hop.

Hailey A. | Chaska, MN

Why don't ants get sick?

Because they have little anty-bodies.

Sydney S. | Antigo, WI

UnitedHealthcare Children's Foundation

Sister: Mom, what can I write for my greatest strength?

Mom: Well, you have a very good memory and that's one of your strengths.

Sister: Oh yeah! I completely FORGOT that I have a good MEMORY!

Vania S. | East Brunswick, NJ

What do giants call stories?

Tall tales.

Sahir S. | El Paso, TX

What's a boulder's favorite music?

Rock and roll.

Marley M. | Parrish, FL

What would you call a flower that loves sun?

A sunflower.

Sruthi K. | Milford, CT

What is the first thing a person does when they get in a pool?

They get wet.

Amber J. | Hacienda Heights, CA

What's a mother pig's story to her baby called?

A pig tale.

Stella R. | Hazelwood, MO

What did the flag say to the pole?

Nothing, it just waved.

Juldyz W. | Buffalo, MN

Knock Knock.

Who's there?

Tickle.

Tickle who?

Tickle Me Elmo.

Neveah B. | Chandler, AZ

Why did the baseball pitcher bring an old pocket watch to his games?

So he could wind up before throwing the ball.

Benjamin D. | Kingwood, TX

How do you get a rhino to stop charging?

You take away its charge card.

Austin L. | Waltham, MA

Where does a fisherman go to get a haircut?

The bobber shop.

Tony W. | Buffalo, MN

What did Ken say to Beach Barbie?

"You're such a doll!"

Cora S. | Eden Prairie, MN

What is a pile of kittens called?

A meow-tain.

Carson M. | Green Bay, WI

What do you call a flying primate?

A hot air baboon.

Henry L. | Woodbridge, VA

Knock Knock.

Who's there?

Some.

Some who?

Summer!

Dexter B. | Huntington, PA

Have you ever tried to eat a clock?

It's very time consuming.

Ethan J. | Las Vegas, NV

A Sasquatch dad comes home after work and tells his Sasquatch wife, "I'm really sad, all of our summer vacation pictures came out blurred."

Alex J. | Hacienda Heights, CA

Knock Knock.

Who's there?

Mommy.

Mommy who?

What? You don't know your own mom?

Asha D. I Monroe, OH

What did the ocean say to the shore?

Nothing, it just waved.

Natalie M. I Apple Valley, MN

Why did the firefly get good grades in school?

He was so bright!

Aspen W. I Rothschild, WI

Why did the chicken cross the road?

To get to the silly goose.

Knock Knock.

Who's there?

The chicken!

Dane R. I Concord, NC

Can bees fly in the rain?

Not without their little yellow jackets.

Cal L. l Woodbridge, VA

How do pirates buy their rings?

With buccaneers.

Sahir S. l El Paso, TX

Why should you tie your shoes?

So they don't run away.

Savannah W. l Chino, CA

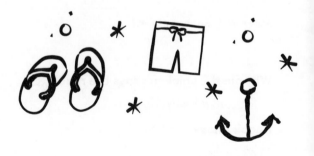

YOU CAN BECOME ONE OF THE AUTHORS!

_____

_____

_____

_____

_____

_____

_____

_____

_____

_____

UnitedHealthcare Children's Foundation

_____

_____

_____

_____

_____

_____

_____

_____

_____

_____

_____

_____

_____

_____

_____

_____

_____

_____

_____

_____

_____

_____

_____

_____

_____

_____

_____

_____

_____

_____

_____

_____

_____

_____

_____

_____

_____

_____

_____

_____

_____

_____

_____

_____

_____

_____

_____

_____

_____

_____

_____

_____

_____

_____

_____

_____

_____

_____

_____

_____

_____

_____

_____

_____

_____

_____

_____

_____

_____

_____

_____

_____

_____

_____

_____

_____

_____

_____

_____

_____

_____

Discover fun
activities and downloads,
when you visit
Oliver & Hope's®
Clubhouse at
vhccf.org/OliverandHope.

FIND OLIVER & HOPE® BOOKS, GIFTS AND MORE AT

vhccf.org/shop

UnitedHealthcare
Children's Foundation